The Temples of Beijing

Foreign Languages Press

SO-AYV-976

The 34.7-m-high Diamond
Throne Pagoda, in Biyun Temple

The Temples of Beijing

Planned by Xiao Xiaoming

Managing editors: Liao Pin, Lan Peijin
Text by Liao Pin, Wu Wen
Photos by Wang Jianhua, He Bingfu, Du Dianwen, Wang Tianxing,
Xie Jun, Sun Shuming, Liu Chungen, Luo Guanglin,
Liu Chen, Wang Xinmin, Wei Xianwen, Yao Tianxing,
Hu Weibiao, Dong Zonggui, Gao Mingyi, Yan Xiangqun,
Lan Peijin, et al.
Translated by Liang Faming
English text edited by Paul White, Wang Mingjie
Cover designed by Wu Tao
Format designed by Yuan Qing, et al.
Edited by Lan Peijin

First Edition 2006

The Temples of Beijing

ISBN 7-119-04388-9

© Foreign Languages Press
Published by Foreign Languages Press
24 Baiwanzhuang Road, Beijing 100037, China
Home Page: http://www.flp.com.cn
E-mail Addresses: info@flp.com.cn
                            sales@flp.com.cn
Distributed by China International Book Trading Corporation
35 Chegongzhuang Xilu, Beijing 100044, China
P.O. Box 399, Beijing, China
Printed in the People's Republic of China

Contents

Statues of deities enshrined in Tianwang (Heavenly King) Hall, the Tanzhe Temple

The Temples of Beijing

"Tanzhe Preceded Youzhou"

The Buddhist temple on Tanzhe Hill on the western outskirts of Beijing is surrounded on the east, west and north sides by nine peaks. In ancient times, the sight was called "nine dragons playing with a pearl" and "a palace hidden in lotus petals." Tanzhe Temple (originally named Jiafu Temple) was built in the Jin Dynasty (265-420). It was the first Buddhist temple built in the Beijing area, a fact reinforced by the common saying: "Tanzhe preceded Youzhou."

The first city built in the location of what is now Beijing was named Ji, and it emerged in about the 11th century BC. When Tanzhe Temple was founded, the city of Ji was the administrative center of Youzhou, a place under the jurisdiction of the united Western Jin Dynasty (265-316), and an important military gar-

Mahavira (great hero) Palace, built on a two-meter-high white stone platform, in Tanzhe Temple

rison in the north. In its heyday, the Tang Dynasty (618-907) devoted great efforts to rebuilding and reinforcing the Ji city walls, and renovating the neighborhoods and government offices. At that time, an alternative name for Ji was Youzhou. Its location is present-day southwest of the urban area of Beijing. Today, some of the ancient streets still remain.

Tanzhe Temple was founded at a time when Buddhism began to spread in Ji, some two centuries after the introduction of Buddhism into China from India via the Silk Road. Legend has it that the spread of Buddhism in China was due to Han Dynasty (206 BC-AD 220) Emperor Liu Zhuang (reigned 58-75). After the Buddha appeared in his dream, he sent envoys to Tianzhu (name for ancient India) in search of the Buddhist scriptures. In Dayueshi or the Kushans (present-day Afghanistan and Central Asia) they encountered two eminent Indian monks, Kashyapa-matanga and Dharmaranya, from whom they acquired Buddhist scriptures and images of the Buddha. They invited the two monks to travel with them back to China. The sacred objects were carried on the back of a white horse. The party reached Luoyang, the Han capital, in the year 67.

The emperor had a temple built in the Indian style on the outskirts of Luoyang for the two Indian monks. It was named White Horse Temple in commemoration of the white horse which had carried the scriptures and the images of Buddha.

The word *si*, which is translated "temple" or "monastery," originally meant a government office. It enjoyed the status next only to the imperial palace. The place where the two monks resided in was deemed as sacred as a *si*. This is how temple came into being.

Building Buddhist Temples and Grottos in Large Scale

The Western Jin Dynasty (265-316) lasted only for half a century, and was wiped out by the Hun of the north in 316. The next year, Sima Rui, a member of the imperial house of the Jin, ascended the throne in Jiankang (present-day Nanjing, Jiangsu Province) and established the Eastern Jin Dynasty (317-420). Since then, China was thrown into endless turbulence and barbarian encroachments. Disappointed and miserable, people turned to the doctrines of "retribution for sin", "transmigration of life and death", "being content with the reality and putting the hope in the next life" advocated by Buddhist preachers. The rulers of the succeeding dynasty, too, patronized the religion, building many temples and carving cliff grottoes as places of worship containing Buddhist statues and devout murals. At the end of the Northern Wei Dynasty (386-534), the number of temples in the north of China had reached more than 30,000. An image of Buddha carved in stone during the Northern Wei Dynasty is still preserved in Beijing's Haidian District. The 2.2 m tall image is one of the oldest stone-carved images of Buddha extant in China. Tianning Temple, located outside Beijing's Guang'an Gate,

Detail of decorative carvings of the pagoda in Tianning Temple

was also built during the Northern Wei Dynasty. It was known as Guanglin Temple at that time.

During the Sui (581-618) and Tang dynasties, when China was united once more, the emperors of the two dynasties energetically supported and promoted Buddhism for the sake of consolidation of their rule, which reached the peak of its influence in China in this period. In the Beijing area a number of leading temples and shrines were built, including Yunju Temple, Hongye Temple (on the basis of Guanglin Temple built in the Northern Wei Dynasty) and Minzhong Temple (present-day Fayuan Temple), as well as the Taoist Tianchang Temple (present-day Baiyun Monastery).

Yunju Temple is situated on the western slope of Mount Shijing, in the southwest of Beijing. During the reign of Emperor Yang (605-617) of the Sui Dynasty, a monk named Jing Wan (?-639) cut grottoes on the hillside, in which he enshrined tablets upon which were carved with the texts of the Buddhist scriptures. Later, he built a temple at the foot of the mountain. Jing Wan's endeavors marked a resurgence of Buddhism after it had been persecuted by two previous emperors. Emperor Taiwu of the Northern Wei Dynasty and Emperor Wu of the Northern Zhou Dynasty (557-581) tried to suppress the religion, and ordered Buddhist monks

Depositary of Buddhist sutra in Fayuan Temple

10

and nuns to resume their secular lives. Hui Si, Jing Wan's master, began to carve scriptures on slabs and hide them in grottos. Before then, Buddhist scriptures had been written on silk and paper which could be easily destroyed. Jing Wan, following Hui Si's footsteps, spent over 30 years carving the scriptures on stone slabs and sealing them in grottos he had excavated by molten iron. After his death, his disciples carried on his work, right up into the 17th century. The 14,278 carved slabs which have survived are considered valuable state treasures.

Fayuan Temple, located outside present-day Xuanwu Gate and built in the Tang Dynasty, is one of the renowned temples of Beijing. In the early Tang Dynasty, Emperor Taizong (reigned 627-649) ordered a Buddhist temple to be built in the Youzhou district to commemorate the dead in an unsuccessful campaign. The building was completed in 696, and given the name Minzhong Temple. According to historical records, there was once a tower known as Minsi inside the temple, but it collapsed in later times, and its exact appearance and dimensions are unknown.

The plain layout of early Chinese temples was patterned upon the Indian model. A pagoda was built at the center of the temple, chiefly for keeping Buddhist relics. Around it were structures for religious service and accommodation for monks. This was the pattern adopted for the White Horse Temple, the first Buddhist temple built in China (in the middle of the 1st century). The main structure was a large square wooden pagoda situated in the center of the temple, encircled by halls, corridors and residences for the monks. Generally, the gate was in the front, and a pagoda was built behind the gate, after which was a hall with an image of Buddha enshrined therein. With the passage of time, this hall assumed equal importance with the pagoda. In the Tang Dynasty, the monk Dao Xuan (596-667) drew up a blueprint for temples which moved the pagoda to the side or back of the main hall.

From the Tang Dynasty, more attention was paid to landscaping, featuring twists and turns which revealed new vistas. While maintaining the pattern of symmetry and unity, scenic spots with garden-like charm were also created within the temple.

"The Number of Temples Ranks First in the North"

In the early 10th century, the Qidan tribe, originated on the Mongolian Plateau, set up the Liao Dynasty (916-1125). The dynasty ruled most of northern China, and in 938 made Youzhou one of its five capitals, with the name Nanjing ("southern capital"). It was also known as Yanjing.

To consolidate the rule, the Liao rulers energetically promoted Buddhism, patronized monks, built temples and pagodas, and had the Buddhist scriptures carved on wooden blocks for printing. Nobles

and wealthy families believing in Buddhism donated large sums of money and land to temples. There

The bronze statue in Leizu Hall in Baiyun Monastery was cast during the Ming Dynasty.

12

were 36 major temples inside the city of Youzhou at that period. However, not many palaces or gardens were built specially for the imperial house for residence and pleasure. According to the *History of Liao Dynasty*, Yanjing was a place where "the number of temples ranks first in the north."

Dajue Temple is located in Yangtai Hill on the western outskirts of the city. Its predecessor was the Qingshui Yuan ("clear water courtyard") Temple, built during the Liao Dynasty. The temple faces east, as the previous one did, which stemmed from a Qidan custom of having buildings face the sun.

The first Beijing mosque was also built during the Liao Dynasty. It was erected in 996 on Niujie Street by an Arabian priest, in an area where Hui (Muslim) people were concentrated. It is the largest extant mosque in Beijing today.

It is said that five pagodas were built around the city during the Liao Dynasty, each marked by a different color. Four of them were destroyed in subsequent wars, and only the White Pagoda of Miaoying Temple, on the inner side of the Fucheng Gate, survived. Ex-

Wangyue Tower inside Niujie Mosque

Yonghe Lamasery

tant pagodas built in the Liao Dynasty are those in Tianning and Yunju temples.

The pagoda was introduced together with Buddhism into China from India. Indian pagodas consist of two kinds: One is for preserving relics of Buddha and eminent monks. It is called stupa, a memorial mound encased in masonry, with an altar and parasol at the top, corridors around the base. There are steps in front of it. The White Pagoda of Miaoying Temple is an example of the structure of this type of pagoda. The other kind is a tower called chaitya built within a grotto. When this type was introduced into China, it evolved into a central tower-post inside a grotto. Buddhist pagodas in China integrated the Indian stupa and the Chinese traditional architecture. The materials used to build pagodas were wood, stone, brick, gold, silver, copper, iron, pottery and glazed ware. They were built in square, round, hexagonal, octagonal and dodecagonal shapes.

The Liao Dynasty was followed by the Jin Dynasty (1115-1234), founded by the Nüzhen tribe. The Jin capital was Yanjing, which was renamed Zhongdu. Under the Jin, a frenzy of temple building took place, and within the capital city alone over 100 new temples and nunneries sprang up. The most famous ones were Mituo Temple, Husheng Temple, Xiangshan Temple, Sheng'an Temple, Long'en Temple, Gongde Temple, Xianglinchan Temple and Que'er Nunnery. Meanwhile, new Taoist temples included those of Yuxu, Tianchang, Chongfu and Xiuzhen.

Famous Temples of the Capital of the Mongol Empire

In 1271, Kublai Khan (1260-1294), ruler of the Mongols, founded the Yuan Dynasty (1271-1368). He spent 20 years building a new city, centered on the northeastern suburb of Zhongdu. The new city was named Dadu. Later he wiped out the Southern Song (1127-1279) and the Jin in 1279 and 1234 respectively and reunited the whole country. From that time up to the present day, Beijing has been the undisputed capital of united China.

Historical records show that Beijing boasted over 1,000 temples during the Ming Dynasty (1368-1644), which succeeded that of the Yuan, and a map of Beijing in the reign of Emperor Qianlong of the Qing Dynasty (1644-1911) shows that there were about 1,400 *hutong* (alleys) in the city, while the number of temples reached more than 1,300, meaning almost one temple in each alley.

Much work went into making some of these temples magnificent structures. For example, in Doulu Temple, expanded at an enormous cost during the Yuan Dynasty, 250 tons of melted copper went into casting a five-meter-long statue of Buddha lying on its side. The temple was then renamed the Recumbent Buddha Temple. Also at that time, sculptures and drawings of high artistic value appeared in large numbers in temples. Masterpieces of the Ming Dynasty include the murals in Fahai Temple in Beijing's Shijingshan District, the colored sculptures in Dahui Temple, the carvings on the foundation of the Diamond Throne Pagoda (five pagodas on a platform) in Wuta Temple and the large exquisite clock in Juesheng Temple outside Xizhi Gate. During the Qing Dynasty, a Diamond Throne Pagoda and replicas of the 500 arhats were added to Biyun Temple (Temple of Azure Clouds).

Taoism thrived alongside the Tibetan form of Buddhism (Lamaism) during the Yuan Dynasty, when the imperial court ordered reduction or exemption of taxes for Taoist temples and their monks and nuns. Taoism was a religion born in China. Laozi, a thinker of the Spring and Autumn Period (770-476 BC), was regarded as the founder of Taoism. What he expounded about Tao in his works was taken as basis of the doctrine of Taoism. Throughout the Yuan and Ming dynasties, Taoism had a huge following, as well as the favor of the court, but it gradually declined in the Qing Dynasty.

For a time, various religions and sects were active in China, and remained so till Qing Dynasty. In the Beijing area, there existed temples and mosques throughout the Yuan, Ming and Qing. Catholic churches began to appear in the Yuan times.

The Taoist Tianchang Temple, built in the eighth century, which changed its name to Changchun Palace in 1227, was later rebuilt over a period of 20 years. Rensheng Palace, built in 1322, was the largest temple of the Orthodox Oneness Sect of Taoism in the whole north China region.

Four famous mosques — Niujie Mosque, Dongsi Mosque, Andingmen Mosque and Jinshifang Mosque — were either built or rebuilt in Beijing during the Ming Dynasty.

Among Lamaist structures, Yonghe Monastery is the most magnificent, having originally been the residence of Qing Emperor Yongzheng (ruled 1723-1735) before he took the throne. The east and west Huangsi temples outside Anding Gate and Zongjing Dazhaozhi Temple in the Fragrant Hill, to the west of the city, were also built during the Qing Dynasty. They all display a mixture of Han Chinese, Tibetan and Indian architectural styles.

Buddhism experienced a rapid decline in modern times, the result of long periods of disunity and warfare. As a consequence, the number of Buddhist temples in Beijing has decreased. Nevertheless, the number of extant temples in and around Beijing still ranks first in the country. They exist side by side with modern buildings and highway overpasses.

Beijing's temples are witnesses to 1,500 years of history. In the past decade or so, the government departments concerned have done a great deal to preserve these monuments of great cultural and esthetic value. Exhibition halls with special themes have been set up inside some of them. For example, the museum of ancient clocks in Juesheng Temple, the exhibition hall of inscribed tablets in Zhengjue Temple, the scripture exhibition hall in Yunju Temple, the art museum in Wanshou Temple and the commercial museum in Baoguo Temple.

The temples of China's capital, no less than the Imperial Palace, Great Wall and Ming Tombs, are among the splendid cultural relics of the Chinese nation; their values and functions have long surpassed the original intentions of their creators. Today, although these temples are still places of worship, they are also sources of information on such subjects as traditional Chinese architecture, sculpture, painting, literature and folk customs. In addition, they are tourist attractions, and the temple fairs and religious festivals they hold have added spice to Beijing residents' lives.

Tanzhe Temple

Built over 1,600 years ago, Tanzhe Temple is one of the most ancient Chinese Buddhist temples. Its original name was Jiafu Temple, and it had the successive names of Longquan (dragon spring), Grand Wanshou (longevity) and Xiuyun (mountain cloud). It got the name Tanzhe from the presence of a pool (*tan*) behind it, and a grove of tree — bristle cudrania (*zhe*) nearby. However, it is not widely known that Xiuyun Temple is the site's official name.

The temple has been repaired and expanded many times throughout the ages, and reached its present dimensions at the end of the 17th century. It covers 6.8 ha, with the main Buddhist temple built at the center, the residence of eminent monks and imperial guests to the east, and a group of scripture halls and shrines to the west. In addition,

Tomb pagodas of the remains of eminent monks and abbots over the past thousand years

1. The Mentougou urban area
2. 6th Ring Road
3. Ten Thousand Buddha Hall
4. Nanxinfang
5. National Highway 108
6. Qiubo
7. Tanzhesi Town

Full view of Tanzhe Temple

Statues of Sakyamuni and his disciples Ananda and Kasyapa

there are the upper and lower pagodas on the slope outside the entrance gate and a meditation room and relaxation pavilion, as well as dragon pool and imperial tablet on the mountainside behind.

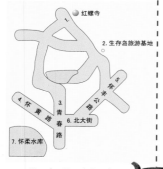

The main entrance gate is built on a slope.

1. Hongluo Temple Road
2. Survival Island, a tourism resort
3. Qingchun Road
4. Huaihuang Road
5. Huaifeng Highway
6. Beida Street
7. Huairou Reservoir

Hongluo Temple

This temple, located in Huairou District on the northern outskirts of Beijing, is 57 km from the city. It was built in 348, during the reign of Ming Emperor Yingzong (1436-1449), when its original name of Daming Temple was changed to Huguo Zifuchan Temple. Legend has it that long, long ago there were two big red conches in the pool on the top of the mountain behind the temple. They gave out an extraordinary light at night. The local

The temple is located at the foot of Mount Hongluo. The picture shows the archway at the entrance.

villagers regarded this as a mystical thing, so they named the mountain and temple "Hongluo" (red conch).

The Mahavira Hall and a pair of ginkgo trees of different sexes, over 1,000 years old, in front of the hall

The temple consists of five courtyards, with the middle courtyard lying horizontally at the foot of Mount Hongluo. In the middle courtyard, arranged from south to north are the entrance gate, Tianwang (Heavenly King) Hall, Mahavira Hall and Sansheng Hall. The east courtyard contains the guest room, kitchen, abbot's quarters and lodgings for visiting monks. Yanshou Hall, by the side of the east courtyard, serves as a retirement home for old monks. At the westernmost end of the temple is a pagoda.

Hongluo Temple was once an important center of the Pure Land Sect of Chinese Buddhism, and attracted a continuous stream of eminent monks seeking enlightenment. Two of the 13 patriarchs of the Pure Land Sect became patriarchs here. Hongluo Temple has also been famous for centuries for its tradition of *qigong* (breath exercises), which are still practiced today.

The Chinese wistaria growing round a pine tree at the back of the main hall is one of the three attractions of the temple.

21

Tianning Temple pagoda is composed of the Sumeru Seat, the 13-eave body and the pinnacle.

Decorations around the Sumeru Seat

Tianning Temple

The predecessor of Tianning Temple was Guanglin Temple, built during the reign of Emperor Xiaowen (471-476) of the Northern Wei Dynasty. The temple was repeatedly destroyed and rebuilt over the centuries, and it bore the names of Hongye Temple, Tianwang Temple and Dawan'anchan Temple until it got its present name in 1435.

Among the existing structures of Tianning Temple, the pagoda behind it is the most magnificent. Rising 57.8 m, it is a solid octagonal brick pagoda of 13 stories built during the Liao Dynasty in the 12th century.

Tianning Temple is located outside Guang'an Gate in the southwest of the urban area of Beijing.

Statue Dating from the Northern Wei Dynasty

A stone image of Buddha erected in 489 during the Taihe Reign of Emperor Xiaowen and located in Che'erying Village near Wenquan in Beijing's Haidian District is the oldest statue of Buddha extant in Beijing. Long ago, there was a temple named Stone Buddha Temple here. Standing 2.2 m tall, the statue is said to have been modeled after the emperor, the seventh emperor of Northern Wei. Rulers of the Northern Wei had been a branch of ancient nationality of Sienpi in north China. Emperor Xiaowen issued

Decorative carvings are seen on all four sides of the pagoda.

1.East Lianhuachi Road
2.North Shoupakou Street
3.Tianning Temple East Street
4.Beibinhe Road, Guang'anmen
5.Guang'anmenwai Avenue
6.Moat

1.Longquan Temple Road
2.Niegezhuang Township
3.Beianhe Road
4.Che'erying Road
5.Qiwangfen Road
6.Phoenix Mountain Scenic Spot

many decrees to promote unity between the Sienpi people with other ethnic peoples, for which he was held in high esteem. On the back of the statue are carved many small statues of Buddha as well as exquisite designs and carvings of a dozen flying *Apsaras* (female musicians).

The statue has a round face and a composed appearance, representing the dignity of the emperor.

Yunju Temple

Yunju Temple, also named Xiyu Temple, is located at the western foot of Shijing (stone-carved scriptures) Mountain, 75 km southwest of the city center. The temple, built in the early 7th century, is famous for its storehouse of 14,278 stone tablets upon which are carved the Buddhist scriptures. These tablets took 1,000 years to complete. Originally, there were six main halls in the temple, arranged in a line from east to west. On both the left and right sides of the main halls were dormitories for the monks, and accommodation for guests and visitors from the imperial court. Most of the temple was destroyed in the 1930s. Reconstruction of the temple is now underway. In 1992, it was among the "Top Ten Tourist Spots of Beijing."

Northern Pagoda built in 711

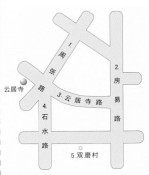

1.Zhouzhang Road
2.Fangyi Road
3.Yunju Temple Road
4.Shishui Road
5.Shuangmo Village

Leiyin Cave, dug in the early 7th century. There are nearly 1,000 Buddhist images carved on four diamond-shaped stone columns in the cave.

The storehouse for stones with carved scriptures was built in 1980. In order to preserve them in a better way, the stones have been put back in the sealed storehouse underground.

Tang Dynasty pagoda

View of Yunju Temple

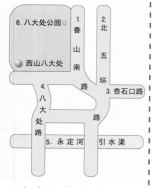

The Yuantong (flexible) Buddhist Hall of Xiangjie Temple

1. South Xiangshan Road
2. North 5th Ring Road
3. Xingshikou Road
4. Badachu Road
5. water diversion channel of the Yongding River
6. Badachu Park

Badachu in the Western Hills

On the western outskirts of Beijing, the Western Hills stretch from north to south. Among the many scenic areas here is the one known as Badachu (eight great sites), referring to eight temples. These temples are located among Mount Cuiwei, Mount Pingpo and Mount Lushi, and the whole area abounds in luxuriant trees and fragrant flowers, springs and exotic rocks.

The eight great sites are Chang'an Temple, Lingguang Temple, Sanshan Nunnery, Dabei Temple, Longwang Hall, Xiangjie Temple, Baozhu Cave and Zhengguo Temple.

They were built from the 7th century to the 17th century. The layouts of the various temples differ from one another, depending on the lie of the mountain, and each has its own attractions, whether pagodas, ornamentation or scenery. They are linked by roads or bridges.

Sanshan Buddhist Nunnery

The Goddess of Mercy Hall of Lingguang (miraculous brightness) Temple

Longquan Nunnery under the shade of pines and cypress

Lingguang Temple pagoda

The Happy Land Memorial Archway in the Pearl Cave

The ancient sala in front of the Great Buddhist Hall of Xiangjie Temple

Dabei Temple

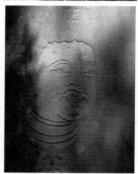

The "Buddha worshipping" tablet of Xiangjie Temple is said to be an ancient Tang Dynasty monument unearthed when the temple was rebuilt during the reign of Emperor Kangxi of the Qing Dynasty. The sunny side of the monument is inscribed with "the true image of the Dabei (infinite mercy) idol." The shady side of the monument is carved with the two words "worshipping Buddha" written by Emperor Kangxi.

Jietai Temple

Jietai (commandment-preaching altar) Temple, situated on Mount Ma'an on the western outskirts of Beijing, is 35 km from the city proper. Built in 622, the temple was then named Huiju Temple. In the 11th century, the eminent monk Fa Jun built the command-ment-preaching altar here to preach the Bud-dhist doctrines, and the temple got its name from the altar.

1. 门头沟地区
2. 六
3. 万佛堂
环
4. 南辛房
路
5. 108 国道
7. 潭柘寺镇 6. 秋波 戒台寺

1.The Mentougou urban area
2.6th Ring Road
3.Ten Thousand Buddha Hall
4.Nanxinfang
5.National Highway 108
6.Qiubo
7.Tanzhesi Town

The temple is a multi-courtyard complex. The main buildings are the Tianwang Hall, Mahavira Hall, Qianfo (thousand Buddha) Hall, Sanxian (three immortals) Hall and Jiuxian (nine immortals) Hall. Situated at the northwest of the temple are Jietai Courtyard, Peony Courtyard, abbot quarters and dormitories for monks. The northeast of the temple is the pagoda compound. The temple is reminiscent of the style of temple common in the area south of the Yangtze River. It is also well known for the stateliness of its pine trees.

The crouching dragon pine was planted during the Liao Dynasty.

The preaching altar of Jietai Temple is the largest one existent in China.

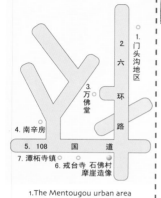

Cliff Carvings in Stone Buddha Village

Stone Buddha Village, in the valley southeast of Jietai Temple, is 35 km from the city proper.

Here on steep cliffs are carved 22 Buddhist images. They are works of the early Ming Dynasty, and include depictions of Manusya, Samantabbhadra,

The four statues in the middle of the north cliff

Mahasthamaprapta, Avalokitesvara, Sakyamuni, Amitabha and Bhaisajyaguru (the Buddha of Medicine). Except the two statues in the shrines at the foot of the cliff, all images of Buddha carved in relief sit on the lotus seat. The tallest is one meter tall, while the others range from 70 to 80 cm. The shapes and postures of the figures are varied, and are skillfully carved.

Statue in the Independent Shrine Cave

The seven statues under the south cliff

Fire God Shrine

Located at No. 77 Di'anmenwai Avenue in Xicheng District, the Fire God Shrine faces the Shrine of the Buddha of Medicine across Qianhai Lake.

The temple was first built in the years 627-649, during the reign of Emperor Taizong of the Tang Dynasty. Its full name is Huode Zhenjun (true lord of the virtue of fire) Shrine. It was rebuilt several times during the Yuan, Ming and Qing dynasties, to reach its present size. The main structures face south, arranged along a north-south axis — front hall, central hall, rear hall, rear pavilion as well as some side buildings including halls of Lord Guan Yu, Jade Emperor, etc. The main gate faces east. The Fire God enshrined in the central hall is a Taoist deity, with red eyebrows and a red beard.

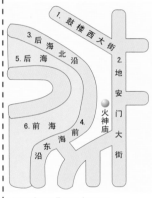

1.West Drum Tower Avenue
2.Di'anmen Avenue
3.The north shore of Houhai Lake
4.The east shore of Qianhai Lake
5.Houhai Lake
6.Qianhai Lake

Entrance gate

Front hall

Wanning Bridge, built in 1285

31

卧佛寺

2. 碧云寺

1.
卧
佛
寺
路

5.

五

3. 香　山　路

4. 香山公园

环

6.
旱
河
路

路

1. Recumbent Buddha Temple Road
2. Biyun Temple
3. Fragrant Hill Road
4. Fragrant Hill Park
5. 5th Ring Road
6. Hanhe Road

Recumbent Buddha Temple

Recumbent Buddha Temple is located at the southern foot of Mount Shou'an on the northwest outskirts of Beijing, about 20 km from the city proper.

Built in the first half of the 7th century, the temple was first named Doulu Temple. Later, it was repeatedly ruined and rebuilt, un-

dergoing several changes of name —
Shouanshan Temple, Dazhaoxiao Temple,
Hongqing Temple and Yong'an Temple. In
1734, at the order of the emperor, it was once
again rebuilt and given the name Shifang
Pujue Temple.

An image of Buddha lying on its side and
carved in sandstone was a feature of the
temple when it was first built. In 1321, this

Statue of Emperor
Qianlong among
statues of arhats

The bronze Recumbent Buddha is 5.2 m
long and weighs 2.5 tons.

Detail of the glazing

Glazed archway

was replaced by a bronze replica.

The architectural pattern of Recumbent Buddha Temple is typical of that of the early Buddhist temples in China, with the entrance gate, Tianwang Hall, Sanshi Buddha (Buddhas of the past, the present and the future) Hall and Recumbent Buddha Hall lying along a north-south axis. On the east and west sides of the axis are the monks' lodgings, and rooms for visitors and imperial guests. Inside the compound of the temple are lotus ponds and well-kept gardens.

Fayuan Temple

Two bronze lions guard Tianwang Hall.

Situated outside Xuanwu Gate in the southwest of the city proper, Fayuan Temple is one of the oldest temples in Beijing, having been built in 696. Its original name was Minzhong Temple. Over the following 1,000 years, it was destroyed and rebuilt several times. In 1442, it was fashioned

34

in its present form, and renamed Chongfu Temple. In the 17th and 18th centuries, emperors of the Qing Dynasty ordered the building of altars and pagodas within the temple. In 1733, it was renovated and got its present name.

The layout of Fayuan Temple is similar to that of Recumbent Buddha Temple. Its six main halls are lined up on a north-south axis. On their sides are auxiliary halls, side rooms and dormitories for monks. The surrounding courtyard is over 180 m long from south to north and 50 m wide from east to west.

The China Buddhism Institute is housed in this temple.

1.Guang'anmennei Avenue
2.Niujie Street
3.Jiaozi *Hutong*
4.Xizhuan *Hutong*
5.Caishikou Street
6.Fayuan Temple Front Street
7.West Nanheng Street

One of the four bronze Tianwang statues that were cast in the 15th century

Stone tablets with inscriptions done at various historical periods

35

Bronze statue of Avalokitesvara (Goddess of Mercy) enshrined on the Great Goddess of Mercy Altar

Interior view of Mahavira Hall

1. National Highway 108
2. Yandong Road
3. Chonglü Road
4. Dongwan Road
5. Shihua Cave

The structure is a three-bay beamless hall with a Chinese hip-and-gable roofs.

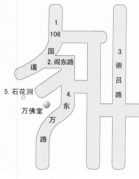

Ten Thousand Buddha Hall

Located at the southern foot of Mount Yunmeng in Fangshan District on the southwest outskirts of Beijing, Ten Thousand Buddha Hall was built in 770, the fifth year of the Dali Reign of the Tang Dynasty. The existing structures date from the Ming Dynasty.

The Hall is a three-bay beamless hall with a hip-and-gable roof and white marble doors and windows, above which are relief sculptures of flying birds and flowers. The "Ten Thousand Bodhisattva Service Map" located in the hall is 23.8 m long and 2.4 m high, and is composed of 31 pieces of rectangular white marble. It dates from the Tang Dynasty.

Relief sculptures on the white marble arch door

Kongshui Cave in the Ten Thousand Buddha Hall

Ten Thousand Buddha Hall and ancient pagoda on the high slope

The four-column, seven-story honorific arch of wooden structure in Baiyun Monastery

1, Fuxingmenwai Avenue
2. Baiyun Road
3. Xibianmenwai Avenue
4. Water diversion channel of the Yongding River
5. Baiyun Monastery Street
6. West Xuanwumen Avenue

Baiyun Monastery

Baiyun (white cloud) Monastery, a famous Taoist temple in Beijing, lies on the southern side of the western section of the straight Chang'an Avenue in the central part of the city proper.

Built in 739, the temple was originally named Tianchang Monastery and was renamed Taiji Palace in 1203. In the 1220s, Emperor Taizu of the Yuan Dynasty, Genghis Khan, ordered Taoist clergyman Qiu Chuji (1148-1227) to take charge of all affairs of Taoism and appointed him abbot of Taiji Palace. Because Qiu Chuji's Taoist name was Changchunzi, hence the palace was renamed Changchun Palace in 1227. It was ruined in war at the end of the 14th century, in the early 15th century, the royal family of the Ming Dynasty ordered reconstruction of

The entrance gate built during the Ming Dynasty

The statue of Laozi, founder of Taoism

the palace. Consequently, it reached its present size and was given the name Baiyun Monastery.

The whole monastery consists of four sections, i.e., the central, east and west routes and the backyard, covering an area of over 10,000 sq m. The six main halls are arranged from south to north of the central route, the side halls, corridors and rooms are arranged respectively on both sides. On the east and west routes stand several independent yet linked courtyards, built inside which are dining-room, pagodas and small halls.

Sanxing (three stars) Hall

The backyard, named Yunji Garden, was built in 1887, inside which are towers, pavilions, terraces and open halls, the three sculptures enshrined in the Mahavira Hall are surrounded by a long corridor, flowers and trees planted here and there, making it a unique garden structure.

Buddha of Medicine Hall

The inner view of Laolü Hall

Eight Immortals Hall

The outer view of Sanqing Hall and Siyu Hall

The 1.16-m-high bronze stove standing in front of Sanqing (three pristine ones) Hall and Siyu (four heavenly ministers) Hall was cast in 1529.

The main hall in the mosque can accommodate 1,000 people for religious service.

Niujie Mosque

A street in the southwestern urban area of Beijing where Hui people are living in compact community is named Niujie Street. Built on the eastern side at the middle section, Niujie Mosque is the largest and most ancient mosque in the region of Beijing.

The mosque was built in 996, buildings in the mosque are in the form of traditional Chinese wooden structure. However, the mosque's general layout and detailed decorations still retain the features of Islamic buildings.

Main structures include the entrance gate, Wangyue Tower, Service Building, Bangke Building, Tablet Pavilion as well as baths.

1. Madao *Hutong*
2. Niujie Street
3. Shuru *Hutong*
4. Jiaozi *Hutong*
5. Chunfeng *Hutong*
6. Shalan *Hutong*
7. West Nanheng Street

41

Though its area is not big, its layout is well-designed, the structure of the halls is varying, its gingerbread is beautiful, compared with Buddhist temples. It achieved the same result with different methods.

According to Islamic religious rules, the believers, when doing religious service, have to face the west to worship the holy place Mecca, that's why the mosque's gate sits in the east but faces the west. The west side of the hall is also honored. And because according to Koran, it is forbidden to use the image of animals as adornment, so the decorative figures of the building are all in the Arabic alphabetic and geometric pattern.

Dajue Monastery

Among a group of peaks in Beijing's Western Hills, there is one looking like a recumbent lion named Yangtai Hill, ancient Dajue Monastery well known in the capital city of Beijing stands on the east slope of the hill.

The monastery was built in 1068, because a clear spring water flows through the

The Great Buddhist Hall inside Dajue Monastery and Longevity Buddhist Hall still retain the architectural style of the Ming Dynasty.

Statues of Buddhas of the past, present and future enshrined in Mahavira Hall

Thousand-year-old ginkgo

1. Qiwangfen Road
2. Xiufeng Temple Road
3. Bei'anhe Road
4. Beiqing Road
5. 6th Ring Road
6. Dajue Temple Road
7. Wenquan Road

whole monastery, hence its name Qingshui (clear water) Temple. Later, it changed its name to Lingquan Monastery. It was renamed Dajue Monastery after its reconstruction in 1428.

The monastery faces east. Entering the entrance gate from the east through the stone bridge, one can reach in proper order Tianwang Hall, Mahavira Hall, Amitayue Hall, Great Mercy Altar through to Sarira (relics) Pagoda built on the hillside. Built on both

A huge stone-carved pond

Longtan

Stone tablet of the Liao Dynasty

sides of main halls are Commandment Altar as well as the south and north Magnolia gardens and Siyi Hall which were built upon the order of the royal family of the Qing Dynasty.

The wonderful view and rare objects honored as the "Six Uniqueness of Dajue," i.e., thousand-year-old ancient stone tablet, Longtan (dragon pool) which collects the inflow of clear water, the ginkgo whose trunk is so thick that needs six people to get their arms around, the white magnolia planted 400 years ago, Baota pine and the pond cut with huge rocks as crystal clear as jade.

Bao Ta (embracing pagoda) pine tree

The inner view of Amitayue Hall

A temple door

Baoguo Monastery

Located on the north of Guang'anmennei Avenue in Xuanwu District, Baoguo Monastery was founded in the Liao Dynasty, which is a thousand-year-old ancient temple. It was destroyed and collapsed in the early Ming Dynasty. In the 2nd year (1466) during the reign of Emperor Xianzong of the Ming Dynasty, it was rebuilt and renamed Ciren Monastery. Again in 1754 during the reign of

Emperor Qianlong, it was reconstructed and changed its name to Grand Baoguo Ciren Monastery, commonly known as Baoguo Monastery.

The monastery, with seven rows of houses, was one of the famous temples in the capital city of Beijing during the Ming and Qing dynasties. Vairochana Tower, 36 stairs in height, in particular, is the most magnificent one. Climbing to the top, one can view palaces, the Western Hills and Lugou Bridge in the capital city of Beijing. They were burned down by the Eight Allied Forces in 1900. The four extant halls still retain their imposing appearance in those years. Existing temples include the imperial tablet set up in the 2nd year of Emperor Xianzong's reign and the poetic tablet of Baoguo Monastery rebuilt in the 21st year during the reign of Emperor Qianlong.

1. Shanguo *Hutong*
2. East Path of Baoguo Monastery
3. Changchun Street
4. Shihu Lane
5. Daxing *Hutong*
6. Guang'anmennei Avenue

The Yuzhi Monument built in the second year under the reign of Emperor Xianzong of the Ming Dynasty

The quite reputed Yuan Dynasty cultural market in the Baoguo Monastery opened up in Beijing.

45

Dayansheng Monastery

Also named Yanshou Monastery and Fahua Monastery, it is located within Changping District in the northwest suburb of Beijing and at the southern foot of Yinshan (silver) Mountain.

First built during the reign of Emperor Da'an (1085-1094) of the Liao Dynasty, it was rebuilt in 1125. When Yansheng Monastery was being built, there were a total of 72 temples and nunneries in Yinshan Mountain, among which Yansheng Monastery is the largest.

For centuries after its completion, the monastery attracted numerous worshippers coming to burn incense and enjoyed equal reputation with Jinshan (gold mountain) Monastery in Zhenjiang, Jiangsu Province, hence the saying: "gold mountain temple in the south and silver mountain temple in the north." After the middle of the 17th century, due to frequent chaos caused by war, few joss-sticks were burnt and the temple gradually became deserted. In the 1940s, as a result of looting and burning by Japanese troops invading China, the monastery was completely destroyed. Among the remaining structures are eminent monks' tomb pagodas which is known as "Yinshan Forest of Pagodas," the name of the monastery has gradually fallen into oblivion.

There are seven extant pagodas in the "Forest of Pagodas," five of which were built

大延圣寺
4. 北庄村
5.
秦
1.
昌
九
3.
2.
赤
长
长
路
6. 定陵
陵
久
镇
路
路
7. 十三陵水库

1. Changchi Road
2. Changling Town
3. Changjiu Road
4. Beizhuang Village
5. Qinjiu Road
6. Dingling Tomb
7. Ming Tomb Reservoir

during the Jin Dynasty in the 12th century, all are dense-eaves brick pagodas. Two are Yuan Dynasty pagodas built in the 13th and 14th centuries.

Miaoying Monastery

There are two famous Tibetan-style white pagodas in Beijing, which are less than 10 km away from each other, Yong'an Monastery White Pagoda is in the east, Miaoying Monastery White Pagoda is in the west. Reputation of the two pagodas is far above that of the monastery.

Miaoying Monastery White Pagoda was built earlier than the monastery. Five colored pagodas were built on five sides of Yanjing city during the Liao Dynasty, but shortly afterwards, they collapsed one after the other. In 1271, Emperor Kublai of the Yuan Dynasty ordered construction of a new pagoda on the old base of the White Pagoda. Construction of the project was placed under the charge of an outstanding Nepalese craftsman Anige, and completed in 1279. After completion

1. Big Tea Leaf *Hutong*
2. Anping Lane
3. Zhao Dengyu Road
4. Gongmenkou East Fork
5. 4th Lane of North Xisi
6. 1st Lane of North Xisi
7. Fuchengmennei Avenue

Changshou Buddha about 5 cm high inlaid in which are 44 rubies and one relic

A bird's-eye view of the monastery

49

Viewing the White Pagoda from the *Hutong* on the eastern side of the monastery

of the pagoda, Kublai ordered people to take the pagoda as the center from which they each shot one arrow to the four sides, then they fixed the site for the monastery at the point where the arrow fell. The monastery covered an area of about 160,000 sq m and was given the name Dashengshou Wan'an Monastery. During the 13th and 14th centuries, the monastery was the place for holding religious activities and translating scriptures in Beijing by the royal family of the Yuan Dynasty.

The monastery was burned down in 1368, rebuilt in 1457 and renamed Miaoying Monastery. At the time of reconstruction, temple halls were all placed in the front of the pagoda. Main buildings include the entrance gate, the Bell-Drum Tower, Tianwang Palace, Yizhu Xinjing Hall, Seven-Buddha Hall, with their area accounting for only one-12th of the original. Today, Miaoying Monastery retains its past-reconstruction pattern, except the entrance gate and Bell-Drum Tower that were demolished.

The inner view of Seven-Buddha Hall

Longquan Monastery

Longquan Monastery, sitting at the foot of Laoye Mountain in Niegezhuang Township of Haidian District on the western outskirts of Beijing, has a history of a thousand years after it was built in the Liao and Jin dynasties. The original monastery, sitting west but facing east, changed its position to the north and faced south during the Qing Dynasty. It is located at the low ridge of a hill, its front faces a mountain stream, above which is a single-span arch bridge. The monastery is arranged in the form of *siheyuan* — a courtyard with houses on four sides, with three compounds standing in a row from west to east. The west compound is the main compound which consists of an entrance hall, a main hall and side halls in the east and west. The main hall is a three-bay house, covering 77 sq m. Exquisite murals are drawn on the walls of the hall. High and steep mountain stands by the side of the temple, beneath the west cliff

A young abbot together with pilgrims

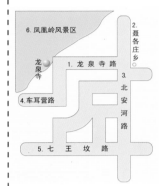

1. Longquan Temple Road
2. Niegezhuang Township
3. Beianhe Road
4. Che'erying Road
5. Qiwangfen Road
6. Phoenix Mountain Scenic Spot

The 1,000-year-old Longquan Monastery is located at the foot of Laoye Mountain.

Jinlong (golden dragon) Bridge with a history of over one thousand years

of the temple is a mountain spring which gurgles down from the mouth of a stone-carved dragon head, putting Longquan in the best situation in those years. Unfortunately, the water level has declined in recent years, and spring water has dried up.

The Buddhist statues of Sakyamuni enshrined in the Great Buddhist Hall

The extant Vajrasana Hall

Huguo Monastery

It is located on Huguo Monastery Street to the northeast of Ping'anli in Xicheng District. Built in the Jin and Yuan dynasties, it was first named Chongguo Monastery. In the fourth year (1429) of the reign of Emperor Xuanzong of the Ming Dynasty, it was re-named Longshan Monastery. In the eighth year (1472) of the reign of Emperor Xianzong of the Ming Dynsty, its name was changed into Dalongshan Huguo Monastery, commonly known as Huguo Monastery. It was rebuilt in the 61st year (1722) under the reign

The glazed parts at the top of the great hall

of Emperor Kangxi of the Qing Dynasty. Its main buildings include Vajrasana Hall, Tianwang Hall, Yanshou Hall, Chongshou Hall, Three Immortals and Thousand Buddha Hall, and Jingming Hall. In the late Qing Dynasty, these buildings were almost all burned down in a conflagration, leaving only Vajrasana Hall and several side rooms untouched.

The only extant Vajrasana Hall is a five-bay one, which is 24.7 m wide and 11.3 m deep, with Chinese hip-and-gable roof with an edge of black glazed tiles and supported by brackets.

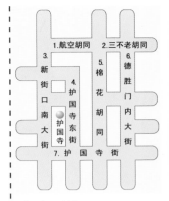

1. Hangkong *Hutong*
2. Sanbulao *Hutong*
3. South Xinjiekou Avenue
4. East Huguo Temple Street
5. Cotton *Hutong*
6. Deshengmennei Avenue
7. Huguo Temple Street

Ruiyun Nunnery, Diamond Pagoda

Located in Che'erying Village, northwest of Niegezhuang in Haidian District on the western outskirts, Ruiyun Nunnery was originally Huangpu Mansion, founded by Emperor Zhangzong (ruled 1190-1208) of the Jin Dynasty. In the 14th year (1501) of the reign of Emperor Xiaozong of the Ming Dynasty, it was changed into Ruiyun Nunnery, now there exists only the ruins.

A huge natural stone, named Diamond stone, stands out on the right side of the entrance gate. The stone, about 20 m high, tilts to one side, hanging above a deep valley, which is too steep to climb. Built on the huge stone is a two-m high, hexagonal, seven-storied, dense-eave brick pagoda, named Diamond Pagoda. It is really a wonderful sight.

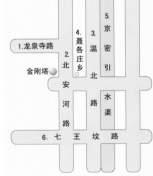

1. Longquan Temple Road
2. Beianhe Road
3. Wenbei Road
4. Niegezhuang Township
5. Beijing-Miyun water diversion channel
6. Qiwangfen Road

The Diamond Pagoda

The ruins of Huangpu Temple, one of the eight great temples in western Beijing

Confucius Temple

Confucius Temple is the temple where Confucius, an ancient Chinese thinker, is worshipped. Confucius (551-479 BC), named Qiu, also styled as Zhong Ni, was a man living in the Spring and Autumn Period. The Confucian School he created advocates rule by virtue, benevolent government, and upholds ethics, Confucius thus won high praise from men of noble of feudal society throughout ages, and honored as master, wise man, sage and is worshipped in temples built in various places.

Confucius Temple in Beijing was built in 1306, its size is only next to the Confucius Temple in Qufu, Shandong, the hometown of Confucius, so Beijing Confucius Temple is the second largest of its kind in China. It is located on the northern side of Chengxian Street (also called Guozijian Street) on the inner side of Anding Gate to the northeast

The archway in Guozijian Street

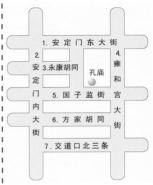

1. East Andingmen Avenue
2. Andingmennei Avenue
3. Yongkang *Hutong*
4. Yonghegong Avenue
5. Guozijian Street
6. Fangjia *Hutong*
7. 3rd Lane of North Jiaodaokou

Dacheng Gate

Making rubbings of portraits of Sage Confucius

A dozen or so hundred-year-old cypress trees are planted in front of Dacheng Hall.

A side view of Dacheng Hall

of the urban area. The temple occupies an area of about 22,000 sq m. Centered at Dacheng Hall, the front side consists of Xianshi Gate and Dacheng Gate; the back side is Chongsheng Memorial Hall enshrined with the memorial tablets of Confucius' ancestors. Outside Dacheng Gate are divine kitchen, Well Pavilion, Slaughter Pavilion, Zhizhai House, and Divine Storehouse, etc. There are 14 tablet pavilions and two "forest of tablets" inside the temple.

White marble cloud-and-dragon relief carvings in front of Dacheng Hall

Books concerning musical performance for worshipping Confucius

Music score for worshipping Confucius during the Ming Dynasty

Musical composition performance staged for worshipping Confucius in the temple

"Forest of Tablets"

One Hundred and ninety-eight pieces of tablets carved with names of successful candidates sitting the imperial examination in the Yuan, Ming and Qing dynasties

Tablet pavilions built by imperial courts throughout ages

Dongyue Temple

Located on the northern side of Chaoyangmenwai Avenue in Chaoyang District, and first built in the 6th year (1319) of the reign of Emperor Renzong of the Yuan Dynasty, this temple is dedicated to the God of Mount Taishan in Shandong Province.

Zhandai Gate

It was the first full-scale temple of the Orthodox Oneness, one of the two main sects of Taoism, in north China. It covers 60,000 sq m, and boasts over 600 halls. The existing buildings were rebuilt during the Qing Dynasty, and the pattern of buildings along the axis still retains the influence of the Yuan Dynasty architecture. The temple complex is divided into the central, eastern and western routes. The central one embraces three-room Jimen Gate, Daiyue Hall and Yude Hall; the eastern one contains Empress Hall and Fumo (subduing demon) God Hall; and the western one embraces Dongyue (Mount

1.North Chaoyangmen Avenue
2.8th Lane of Jishikou
3.North Chaowai Street
4.East Jishikou Street
5.Jishikou *Hutong*
6.Yangjia *Hutong*
7.Chaoyangmenwai Avenue

The glazed archway in front of the temple

Taishan) Hall, Yuhuang (Jade Emperor) Hall and Buddha of Medicine Hall. The temple houses 30 stones carved during the Yuan, Ming and Qing dynasties.

Inscribed steles kept in the temple

Dongyue Temple

康熙御筆

東嶽廟

Daiyue Hall

Lord Bingling Hall (Bingling was said to be the third son of God Dongyue)

Vertical board inscribed with the calligraphy of Emperor Kangxi

Touching the Tongtie in Dongyue Temple was a custom thought to cure diseases. The tongtie is a mythical beast with a horse's head, a mule's body, a donkey's tail and an ox's feet. It is said to be the chair of God Wen Chang

"Stele of Priest Zhang Liusun" written by Zhao Mengfu (1254-1322), a leading calligrapher of the Yuan Dynasty

Internal view of Yude Hall

Yude Hall

Cibei Nunnery

Avalokitesvara Hall

Located on a terrace on the Central Isle in Taoran Park in Xuanwu District, and also called Avalokitesvara Nunnery, Cibei (mercy) Nunnery was built in the Yuan Dynasty. It was repeatedly renovated in the Ming and Qing dynasties, resulting in the present layout. On the temple gate are carved the characters meaning "Ancient Temple of Mercy."Inside the gate there is a wooden board bearing the words "Tao Ran" inscribed by Jiang Zao, an official of the Ministry of Works during the reign of Qing Emperor Kangxi. The nunnery preserves steles with passages from the Buddhist scriptures, images of Buddha and incantations inscribed on all four sides of them, dating from the Liao Dynasty.

The Avalokitesvara Nunnery was rebuilt in the second year (1663) under the reign of Emperor Kangxi. The two pieces of stones

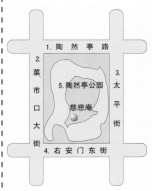

1.Taoranting Road
2.Caishikou Avenue
3.Taiping Street
4.East Youanmen Street
5.Taoranting Park

Cibei Nunnery

Zhunti Hall

Open-work carvings of the image of Buddha on the Jin Dynasty scripture stone tablet

The place where revolutionaries had their activities there in modern times

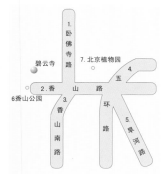

carved with "Notes on Tao Ran Pavilion" and "Ode to Tao Ran" are inlaid on the southern wall of the Open Pavilion. The nunnery also houses a cultural relics exhibition displaying cultural relics about revolutionaries' activities in Tao Ran Pavilion in modern times.

Scripture stone tablet of the Liao Dynasty

Biyun Temple

Situated at the eastern foot of the Fragrant Hill, this temple was originally the private mansion of a Yuan Dynasty official. In 1289, it became Biyun Nunnery. It was expanded twice, in 1516 and 1623, respectively, by the court eunuchs Yu Jing and Wei Zhongxian, and its name was changed first to Yugong Temple and then Biyun (azure cloud) Temple.

The central part of the temple embraces five halls, standing one above the other on

1. Recumbent Buddha Temple Road
2. Fragrant Hill Road
3. South Fragrant Hill Road
4. 5th Ring Road
5. Hanhe Road
6. Fragrant Hill Park
7. Beijing Botanical Garden

The stone archway in front of the Diamond Throne Pagoda

over 100 m of the mountain slope. At the highest point behind the temple is Diamond Throne Pagoda built in 1748, and on the southern side of the temple is a hall for the worship of the arhats, also built in 1748. On the northern side of the temple are Shuiquan Compound and Bihan Zhai Studio.

Scripture stone stele and bronze cooking vessel dating from the mid-Qing Dynasty in the front of Mahavira Hall

Interior view of Mahavira Hall

Statue in front of the tomb of Ming Dynasty eunuch Wei Zhongxian at Biyun Temple

Arhat Hall

Biyun Temple in snow

Guanghua Temple

This temple is located on the eastern bank of Shishahai Lake, close to Di'an Gate. Built in the Yuan Dynasty, it underwent three periods of reconstruction, in the 16th century and twice in the 19th century, respectively. The buildings are built along five routes.

Guanghua Temple preserves valuable ancient editions of *The Tripitaka Sutra*, *Dai Nippon Zoku Zokyo* (Supplement to the Tripitaka, Japanese edition) and other rare editions of Buddhist sutras.

The temple is also the headquarters of the Beijing Buddhist Association.

1. West Drum Tower Avenue
2. Ya'er *Hutong*
3. North shore of Houhai Lake
4. Houhai Lake
5. South shore of Houhai Lake

One of the scripture stone tablets newly erected outside the entrance gate

Statue of Skanda

Tianwang Hall

Two inscribed stone tablets dating from the Ming Dynasty

Wooden Fish

Amitabha Hall

Buddha of Medicine Hall

Interior view of
Five-Buddha Hall

Five-Buddha Hall

Zhenjue Temple

The temple is located outside Xizhi Gate in downtown Beijing. The Changhe River, with ancient willows on both banks, flows from northwest to southeast through the city. The banks of the river witnessed busy religious activities during the 15-19 centuries in Beijing.

This temple was founded in the Yongle reign (1403-1424) of Emperor Chengzu of the Ming Dynasty, and renamed Grand Zhengjue Temple in 1761. Since the building of the Diamond Throne Pagoda (one made of five pagodas on a base) in the compound, it was called Five-Pagoda Temple.

The main structure is the Diamond Throne Pagoda, built in 1473. It is one of only ten pagodas built in this style in China. Four of them are in Beijing, the other three being at Biyun Temple, Xihuang Temple and Miaogao Temple.

Statue of Jun Jue of the Eastern Han Dynasty (25-220), who was sent as an envoy to the Western Regions

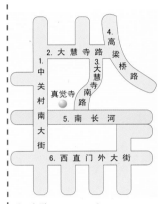

1. South Zhongguancun Avenue
2. Dahui Temple Road
3. South Dahui Temple Road
4. Gaoliang Bridge Road
5. South Changhe River
6. Xizhimenwai Avenue

Buddha images are carved on all four sides of the base of the pagoda.

Stone trough of the Ming Dynasty

Decorative carvings on the body of the pagoda

69

Statue made in the 23rd year (499) of the Taihe Reign of Emperor Xiaowen of the Northern Wei Dynasty

Statues in the tomb passage

Diamond Throne Pagoda

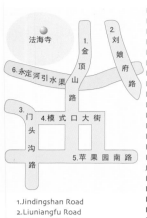

Mural of Virupaksha,
Guardian King of the
West, on the western
side of the northern
wall of Mahavira Hall

Fahai Temple

Located at the southern foot of Mount Cuiwei in Shijingshan District on western outskirts of Beijing, the temple is famous for its superb Buddhist murals.

The temple was built with funds raised by Li Tong, a eunuch of the Ming Dynasty. Construction started in 1439, and the temple and its murals were completed simultaneously after four years. Originally, the temple included Tianwang Hall, Sangharama Hall, Dharmapala Diamond Hall, Mahavira Hall, Patriarch Hall, and the Bell and Drum towers. Only Mahavira Hall and its murals have

Mural of Sovereign Sakra (detail)

The internal view of the Tianwang Hall

withstood the wear and tear of the ages; the others have been reconstructed in recent years.

The Mahavira Hall murals cover an area of 236.7 sq m, including murals of *Gods Paying Homage to Buddha*, *Wonderland of Five Buddhas*, flying *Apsaras*, *Avalokitesvara Gazing at the Moon Reflected in the Water*, Manjusri and Samantabheadra. There are more than 70 figures, executed with traditional Chinese brush strokes and in bright colors and meticulous style, including the technique of using gold for coloring. Done by court painters, they are said to be the best Ming Dynasty murals in China.

Mahavira Hall

Zhihua Temple

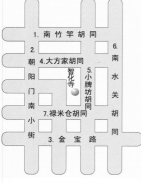

The stone lion outside the temple door

1. Nanzhugan *Hutong*
2. Nanxiaojie Street, Chaoyangmen
3. Jinbao Road
4. Dafangjia *Hutong*
5. Xiaopaifang *Hutong*
6. Nanshuiguan *Hutong*
7. Lumicang *Hutong*

The temple door

Located at the eastern entrance of Lumicang *Hutong*, a densely inhabited ancient lane in Dongcheng District, Zhihua Temple was built in 1443. It was originally a family temple built by eunuch Wang Zhen, who was in charge of protocol, of the Ming Dynasty. Only six years after the completion of the temple, Wang Zhen was put to death due to court intrigue, and the temple was confiscated and turned into public property.

The architectural pattern strictly follows the shape and structure of ancient Chinese temples. All buildings are grouped along three routes. The central one is in turn divided into the front, middle and back yards. The front yard embraces seven halls, the middle yard has only Tathagata Hall, and in the back yard are the Hall of Great Mercy and the Hall of Ten Thousand Buddhas. Beside the entrance gate are the eastern side gate and the western side gate. The long passage behind the western gate leads to the abbot's quarters while the passage behind the eastern gate leads to the back temple.

Preserved in the temple are 10 editions of the *Tripitaka Sutra* dating from the 18th century. The printing blocks were carved at the order of Qing Emperor Qianlong, and this set is known as the *Tripitaka, Qianlong Edition*.

The turning wheel inside the wheel-turning hall

A copper cast auspicious beast

Zhihua Buddhist Hall

Mural paintings of the Ming Dynasty

The ancient engraved Buddhist sutra plate collected in the Beijing Wenbo Exchange Hall inside the Zhihua Temple

The Ten Thousand Buddha Pavilion of the Tathagate Buddhist Hall

Long'an Temple

Situated at Baiqiao Nanli on the inner side of Guangqu Gate in Chongwen District, the temple was built in the fifth year (1454) of the Jingtai Reign of Emperor Daizong of the Ming Dynasty and was rebuilt in the 37th year (1609) of the Wanli Reign of Emperor Shenzong. The extant buildings are the entrance gate, Tianwang Hall, front hall, big hall and back hall. There are also four stone tablets, one of which was erected in the fifth year of the reign of Emperor Daizong. Growing in the temple are two *catalpa bungeis*, rarely seen in Beijing, which form a delightful contrast with two cypresses in front of the temple, which are about 700 years old.

1.Beibinhe Road, Guangqumen
2.Baiqiao Avenue
3.Moat
4.Nanbinhe Road, Guangqumen
5.Guangqumennei Avenue

The Long'an Temple door

Guangji Temple

Guangji Temple, one of the famous ancient Buddhist temples in Beijing, was built in the Jin Dynasty (1115-1234).

Originally known as Xiliucun Temple, it collapsed and was forgotten until the 15th century, when local people discovered relics of it while digging. During the Tianshun Reign of Ming Emperor Yingzong (1436-1450), monk Pu Hui and his disciple Yuan Hong raised money for its reconstruction. The project gained support from the imperial

Signboard with Emperor Kangxi's calligraphy on the entrance gate

77

1. 平安里西大街
2. 翠花街
3. 赵登禹路
4. 西四北四条
5. 西四北大街
6. 西四北头条
广济寺
7. 阜成门内大街

1. West Ping'anli Avenue
2. Cuihua Street
3. Zhao Dengyu Road
4. 4th Lane of North Xisi
5. North Xisi Avenue
6. 1st Lane of North Xisi
7. Fuchengmennei Avenue

Bronze statue of Bodhisattva Skanda

The exquisite, long-year musical instrument of the Buddhist circle

family, and was given the name Hongci Guangji Temple.

The main buildings of the temple are the entrance gate, Tianwang Hall, Mahavira Hall, Yuantong Hall, Hall of Buddha of Abundant Treasures and Scripture Library, as well as the Commandment Altar, an additional structure built in the late 17th century.

Stored in the temple are over 100,000 copies of sutras, including a whole set of the Ming Dynasty edition of the *Tripitaka Sutra*. In addition, there are more than 30,000 stone sutra rubbings from Yunju Temple in Fangshan District, relics of Dharmacarya (Master of the Law), as well as many inscribed steles and other Buddhist cultural relics.

The China Buddhism Association and the Chinese Buddhist Research Institute are housed in the temple.

Bronze statue of Maitreya

Yuantong Hall

The Gooddess of Mercy enshrined in the
Yuantong Hall

The Great Buddhist Hall

Interior of Mahavira Hall

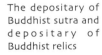

The depositary of
Buddhist sutra and
depositary of
Buddhist relics

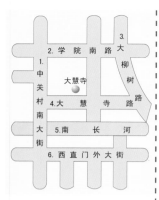

Dahui Temple

Located at Daliushu Beicun outside Xizhi Gate, this temple, built in 1513, is about one km from Zhenjue Temple.

Hall of Great Mercy is the only extant building. Originally, there was a 16-m-high bronze Buddha in the temple, which also bore the name Great Buddha Temple, but it was destroyed by Japanese invaders in the 1940s. Fortunately, another statue of Buddha and murals are still well preserved.

The temple has 28 statues of Devas of

Colored statues of deities

Law Protection, executed in the 16th century. The statues are all three meters high color sculptures, standing on the seat of Sumeru and almost touching the ceiling of the hall.

On the inner walls of the hall is a group of colored pictures, describing the progress of a man who, through good deeds and the help of Buddha, attained Nirvana.

Hall of Great Mercy, built in the architectural style typical of the Ming Dynasty

Detail of the mural

Colored statues of Buddha on a wooden base

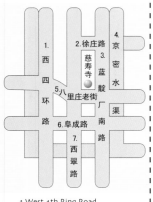

1. West 4th Ring Road
2. Xuzhuang Road
3. South Landianchang Road
4. Beijing-Miyun water diversion channel
5. Balizhuang Old Street
6. Fucheng Road
7. Xicui Road

Cishou Temple

Situated at Balizhuang outside Fucheng Gate, this temple is four km from the city center.

It was built by Empress Dowager Li in the fourth year (1576) of the Wanli Reign of Emperor Shenzong of the Ming Dynasty. As Shenzong was only ten years old when he came to the throne, the empress dowager acted as regent. A devout Buddhist, she had many Buddhist places of worship built or repaired. Cishou Temple was one of them.

Only a pagoda — Yong'an Wanshou Pagoda — remains, said to have been built on the pattern of Tianning Temple Pagoda. Typical of the Ming Dynasty style of pagoda architecture, this brick pagoda is 50 m high and has 13 stories. It is octagonal in shape, with dense eaves. The decorations on the base, body and eaves are finely wrought.

Yong'an Wanshou Pagoda

Wanshou Temple

One km west of Zhenjue Temple, along the Changhe River, is Wanshou (longevity) Temple. Wanshou Temple was built in 1578 after Cishou Temple by Empress Dowager Li, mother of Emperor Shenzong of the Ming Dynasty. In 1751 and 1761, Emperor Qianlong, in order to celebrate the birthday of his mother, twice repaired and expanded Wanshou Temple, making it an integrated complex of a temple, gardens and palace for the emperor's temporary stay when away from home.

The temple is divided into three sections: The middle one is composed of the entrance gate, Tianwang Hall, Mahavira Hall, Wanshou Tower, Dachan Hall, Bodhisattva Hall and Amitayus Hall arranged in order from south to north; the eastern section is the abbot's quarters; and the western section is the imperial quarters.

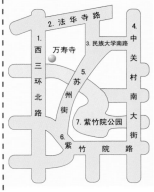

The tablet pavilion of Emperor Qianlong and Amitayus Hall

1. North Section, West 3rd Ring Road
2. Fahua Temple Road
3. South Nationalities University Road
4. South Zhongguancun Avenue
5. Suzhou Street
6. Purple Bamboo Park Road
7. Purple Bamboo Park

Exterior view of Wanshou Temple

Gilt bronze statue of
Vairocana in Mahavira Hall

When the emperors and empresses of the Qing Dynasty made an excursion by waterway to the Summer Palace and Western Hills, they went ashore at Guangyuanzha, to the east of Wanshou Temple. They burned incense and worshipped Buddha in Wanshou Temple before continuing their journey in another boat.

Courtyard gate in a combination of Chinese and foreign styles (the latter in French Baroque style)

The Buddha of Medicine

In Amitayus Hall there is a gold-mixed bronze Buddhist pagoda cast in 1621. There are over 400 sculptures, including ones of Buddha, Bodhisattva and arhat, carved on the body of the pagoda.

Exterior view of Mahavira Hall

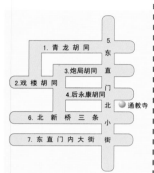

1. 青龙胡同
2. 戏楼胡同
3. 炮局胡同
4. 后永康胡同
5. 东直门北小街
6. 北新桥三条
7. 东直门内大街
通教寺

1. Qinglong *Hutong*
2. Xilou *Hutong*
3. Paoju *Hutong*
4. Houyongkang *Hutong*
5. Beixiaojie Street, Dongzhimen
6. 3rd Lane of Beixinqiao
7. Dongzhimennei Avenue

Tongjiao Temple

Statue of Ksitigarbha

Situated on the inner side of the Dongzhi Gate in the east of the city, this temple was originally built by a eunuch of the Ming Dynasty and reconstructed into a nunnery named Tongjiao in the Qing Dynasty. In 1942, the nuns Kaihui and Shengyu, coming from Fujian to Beijing, collected money to repair and expand the temple, and renamed it Tongjiao Temple.

The expanded Tongjiao Temple covers an area of 2,500 sq m, and includes the entrance gate, Mahavira Hall, Guardian Deity Hall, Patriarch Hall, dining-room and monks' and nuns' dwellings.

The number of nuns and monks was about 70 at its heyday. Tongjiao Temple has always been known for its strict adherence to monastic rules.

Interior view of Mahavira Hall

Cishan Temple

Located on the terrace halfway up Tiantai Mountain in Shijingshan District on the western outskirts of Beijing, this temple was built in the Ming Dynasty.

It is divided into the central, east and west areas, with Hall of Great Mercy in the west area as the main attraction. A lacquered wooden statue of Avalokitesvra is enshrined in the hall, flanked by eight other statues, including Goddess Pixia. Buddhist and Taoist figures in the same hall is a rare sight in Beijing's temples.

Temple Entrance Hall.

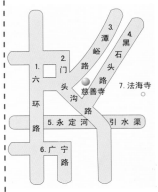

1.6th Ring Road
2.Mentougou Road
3.Tanyu Road
4.Heishitou Road
5.water diversion channel of the Yongding River
6.Guangning Road
7.Fahai Temple

View of the temple

Pudu Temple

Located on the eastern side of northern end of Nanchizi Street in Dongcheng District, this temple stands on the site of the God of the North Pole of the Yuan Dynasty which was later used as the site of Hongqing Palace of the Ming Dynasty. In the early Qing Dynasty, it was renovated as a palace for Prince Regent Dorgon (1612-1650) and

Temple entrance

known as the Imperial Palace of Prince Rui. In the 33rd year (1694) of the reign of Emperor Kangxi, it was rebuilt as Maha Gela (big black god) Temple. It was rebuilt in the 40th year (1775) of the reign of Emperor Qianlong, and renamed Pudu Temple.

The only extant building of Pudu Temple is the nine-bay Ciji Hall, standing on a white marble Sumeru Seat, covered with open work of acanthus and lotus designs. There are 36 columns on the four sides. The three-eave-roof of its veranda is covered with green glazed tiles with an edge of yellow glazed tiles.

The renovated Pudu Temple

The temple is built on the high terrace. It is said that in the past there was a concealed path leading directly to the Imperial Palace.

Three storied heavy eave-structures are rare in traditional Chinese buildings.

Ciji Hall

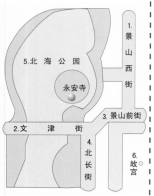

Yong'an Monastery

This monastery is located on the southern slope of Qionghua Islet in Beihai Park. The islet has been an imperial garden since the 11th century. In 1651, on the site of a ruined hall of the previous dynasty, a Tibetan-style white pagoda was built. A monastery was built later in front of the pagoda, and since then Qionghua Islet has been known as White Pagoda Hill and the monastery as White Pagoda Monastery. After it was rebuilt in 1743, it was formally named Yong'an Monastery.

The White Pagoda is located in the cen-

View of Yong'an
Monastery

ter of the islet, facing south. It is the highest point of Yong'an Monastery. Shanyin Hall, Pu'an Hall, Zhengjue Hall, Dharma Hall, entrance gate and the archway extend south one after the other.

The islet is linked to the shore by Yong'an Bridge.

The roof of all the major structures of the monastery is covered with yellow and green glazed tiles. The roof ridge of the halls is in the form of a dragon. Exotic stones, pavilions and platforms arranged around the monastery give the islet the appearance of an imperial palace.

Shanyin Hall in front of the White Pagoda is a glazed wooden structure.

Interior view of the main hall

Yonghe Lamasery

In 1694, Emperor Kangxi of the Qing Dynasty had a luxurious and imposing residence built at Andingmen in the northeast of Beijing for his fourth son, Yinzhen. Twenty-eight years later, Yinzhen succeeded to the throne as Emperor Yongzhen (reigned 1723-1735), and moved into the Forbidden City. Half of his old residence was given to monks

Central Hall of Yonghe Lamasery

of Gelugpa Sect (or Yellow Sect), and the other half was used as a temporary lodging for the emperor.

Not long afterwards, a fire destroyed part of the structure used as a temporary lodging for the emperor. The remaining buildings were named Yonghe Palace in 1725, and they formally became a lamasery in 1744.

Because the predecessor of Yonghe Lamasery was an imperial palace, its architectural pattern is different from those of other temples. It is more or less like an imperial palace. The main gate faces south. On the 480-m-long axial line extending from south to north are a decorated archway, Zhaotai Gate, Tianwang Hall, Central Hall, Yongyou Hall, Dharma Hall, Wanfu

Decorated archway

Pavilion and Suicheng Building. The place is nearly 120 m wide from east to west. Flanking the main buildings are the Bell and Drum towers, Tablet Pavilion, Tantrism Hall,

The outer view of Dharma (the wheel of the law) Hall

Sutra Preaching Hall, Mathematics Hall and Buddha of Medicine Hall, Panchen Building, Commandment Altar, Zhaofo Building, Yamudaga Building, Yongkang Pavilion, Yansui Pavilion, eastern and western Shunshan buildings, and eastern and western side halls.

Interior of Dharma Hall

The silver Commandment Altar in the lamasery's collection

The bronze sumeru pedestal cast during the years under the reign of Emperor Shenzong of the Ming Dynasty

Statue of Emperor Qianlong as a Buddha

White sandstone Buddha statues

94

Statue of Buddha 18-m high carved from a single tree trunk in Wanfu Pavilion

Tripitaka Sutra

Statue of Bde-mchog-rdo-rje

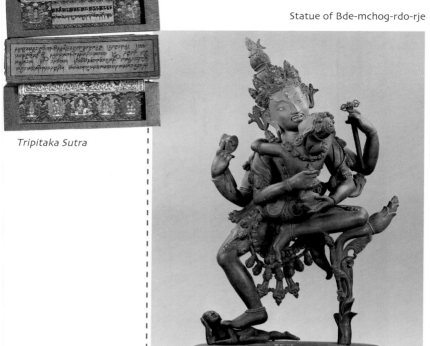

Wanfu Pavilion

Xihuang Temple

This Gelugpa Lamaist temple is situated outside Anding Gate in the northern part of the urban area of Beijing. It was built in 1652. This sect is also called the Yellow Sect, because the monks wear yellow hats and robes. So the temple is also known as the Yellow Temple.

To the east, there used to be another Tibetan Buddhist temple, built in 1651 and known as the East Yellow Temple, to distinguish it from Xihuang (West Yellow) Temple. The former has long since vanished.

In 1780, when the Sixth Panchen Lama, Dadain Yexe (1738-1780), came from Tibet to Beijing to congratulate Emperor Qianlong on his birthday, he stayed in this temple. Later in the same year, the Panchen Lama died in Beijing. Emperor Qianlong ordered a stone

Wall decorations in Chinese and Tibetan styles

1.Central Section, North 3rd Ring Road
2.Deshengmenwai Avenue
3.Huangsi Avenue
4.Gulouwai Avenue
5.Jiaochangkou Street
6.Ande Road
7.East Deshengmen Avenue

Qingjinghua Pagoda

Stone carvings on the four walls of the Qingjing Huacheng
Pagoda are all drawings of Buddha Sakyamuni.

pagoda to be built to the north of the temple to preserve the holy man's remains and named it Qingjinhua Pagoda. The stone pagoda bears traces of Indian, Tibetan and Chinese architectural styles. It is still well preserved.

The Tibetan Buddhism Institute is housed in the temple, which receives leading Tibetan and Mongolian monks for advanced studies all the year round.

The renovated entrance gate

Teachers and students of the Tibetan Language Department of the Advanced Buddhism Institute inside the Great Buddhist Hall are engaged in Buddhist ceremonies.

Fuyou Temple

Situated on the east side of the north end of Beichang Street of Xicheng District, this temple was built during the reign of Emperor Shizong (1644-1661) of the Qing Dynasty. Originally it was a

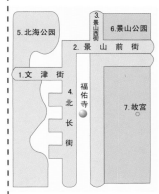

place for avoiding smallpox, and served as a private school for Shizong's son Xuanye (later Emperor Kangxi). In the first year (1723) of the reign of Emperor Yongzheng, the place was converted into a Tibetan Buddhist temple, and named Fuyou Temple.

The temple faces south. The gate of the outer enclosure wall, situated in the southwest corner, faces west. On the axial line, from south to north, are a screen wall, decorated archway, entrance gate, Bell and Drum towers, Tianwang Hall, Mahavira Hall and back hall. The horizontal boards over the decorated archway and the main hall bear the calligraphy of Emperor Yongzheng. After the founding of the People's Republic of

Detailed decoration of the archway

1.Wenjin Street
2.Jingshan Front Street
3.West Jingshan Street
4.Beichang Street
5.Beihai Park
6.Jingshan Park
7.Imperial Palace

Fuyou Temple

China in 1949, the office of the Panchen Lama's representative in Beijing was set up in this temple.

The rear hall of Fuyou Temple

The Green Saviouress statue enshrined in the Great Buddhist Hall of Fuyou Temple

Fuyou Temple in snow

The Guardian King of the South statue in the Tianwang Hall of Fuyou Temple, which is the only statue not repaired and preserving the original color in the Ming Dynasty temples in the Beijing region

Entrance gate

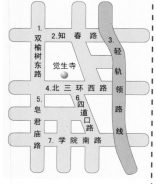

1. East Shuangyushu Road
2. Zhichun Road
3. light railway line
4. West section, North 3rd
   Ring Road
5. Zaojun Temple Road
6. Sidaokou Road
7. South Xueyuan Road

Juesheng Temple

Juesheng Temple, commonly known as Big Bell Temple, is situated on western section of North 3rd Ring Road. It was first built in 1733, when the place was far away from the city and secluded.

The layout of the temple is strictly symmetrical. Arranged from south to north are the screen wall (already collapsed), the entrance gate, Tianwang Hall, Mahavira Hall, Avalokitesvara Hall, Sutra Library and Big Bell Tower. The abbot's quarters are located on the east side of the temple.

The Big Bell was moved here from Wanshou Temple in 1743, during the reign of Emperor Chengzu of the Ming Dynasty.

Detail of the Big Bell

The Big Bell is 6.94 m high and weighs 46.5 tons.

One of the exhibition rooms displaying ancient bells

Bell cast in 1627 by the treasonous minister Wei Zhongxian

Bell with dragon design cast during the reign of Ming Emperor Xianzong (1465-1488)

Big Bell Tower

The bell was cast in the years under the Yongle Reign of Emperor Chengzu (1403-1424). It bears over 100 kinds of Chinese and Sanskrit incantations and inscriptions, running to as many as 230,000 words inside and outside.

In 1985, a bell museum was opened in the temple.

Emperor Worship Temple

This temple is situated on the inner side of Fucheng Gate in the west of the urban area of Beijing and less than one km from the White Pagoda of Miaoying Temple. The temple was completed in 1531. Up until the fall of the last dynasty, the Qing, in 1911, it was the place to worship emperors and famous ministers of the past. Enshrined in the temple are 188 spirit tablets of emperors — from the legendary Three Emperors and Five Sovereigns down to the last emperor of the Ming Dynasty (Sizong, reigned 1628-1644). The tablets are enshrined in five rooms of the main hall, known as Jingde Sage-wor-

1. Big Tea Leaf *Hutong*
2. Anping Lane
3. Zhao Dengyu Road
4. Gongmenkou East Fork
5. 4th Lane of North Xisi
6. 1st Lane of North Xisi
7. Fuchengmennei Avenue

Spirit tablets of emperors preserved in the Jingde Sage-worshipping Hall

107

Jinde Sage-worshipping Hall

shipping Hall.

In the rooms on both sides of the hall are enshrined the spirit tablets of 79 meritorious ministers.

From the 1930s to the end of the 20th century, the temple was used as a school. It has now been renovated and opened to the public.

Spirit tablets of 30 emperors of the Jin, Yuan and Ming dynasties

The magnificent layout demonstrates the grandeur of imperial house shrines.

Emperor Qianlong's calligraphy on the back of a stele in the Southwest Stele Pavilion

Southeast Stele Pavilion

Dongliao Stove

Exhibition of
P r o m i n e n t
Emperors

Sage-worshipping Hall is one of the key monuments
ultural relics under the national protection.

图书在版编目（CIP）数据

北京寺庙道观／肖晓明策划，廖频、兰佩瑾编.
－北京：外文出版社，2006
（漫游北京）

ISBN 7-119-04388-9

Ⅰ．北… Ⅱ．①肖… ②廖… ③兰… Ⅲ．寺庙-简介-北京市-
英文 Ⅳ．k928.75

中国版本图书馆 CIP 数据核字(2006)第 017581 号

策　　　划：肖晓明

编　　　辑：廖　频　兰佩瑾
撰　　　文：廖　频　吴　文
摄　　　影：何炳富　杜殿文　望天星　谢　军　孙树明　刘春根
　　　　　　罗广林　刘　臣　王新民　韦显文　姚天星　胡维标
　　　　　　董宗贵　王建华　高明义　严向群　兰佩瑾等
翻　　　译：梁发明
英 文 定 稿：Paul White　王明杰
封 面 设 计：吴　涛
版 式 设 计：元　青等
责 任 编 辑：兰佩瑾

北京寺庙道观

© 外文出版社
外文出版社出版
（中国北京百万庄大街 24 号）
邮政编码：100037
外文出版社网页: http://www.flp.com.cn
外文出版社电子邮件地址: info@flp.com.cn
sales@flp.com.cn
北京外文印刷厂印刷
中国国际图书贸易总公司发行
（中国北京车公庄西路 35 号）
北京邮政信箱第 399 号 邮政编码 100044
2006 年 8 月(长 24 开)第 1 版
2006 年第 1 版第 1 次印刷
（英）
ISBN 7-119-04388-9
005800（平）
85-E-628P